Serge Prokofieff

PETER AND THE WOLF

A musical tale for children

PIERRE ET LE LOUP

Conte symphonique pour enfants

PEDRO Y EL LOBO

Cuento sinfónico para niños

Arranged for piano solo by Thomas F. Dunhill
Illustrations by Peter Bailey

Texte français de Raymond Gérôme
Texto español por Juan Serrallonga

Boosey & Hawkes Music Publishers Ltd
www.boosey.com

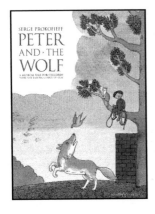

Also available:
Peter and the Wolf children's book,
arranged for easy piano by Carol
Barratt, with the story retold in
verse and illustrated in full colour.

ISMN M 060 11214 0
ISBN 0 85162 269 0

Each character in this tale is represented by a different musical theme and, in performances with orchestra, by a different instrument: the bird by the flute, the duck by the oboe, the cat by the clarinet, the grandfather by the bassoon, the wolf by three horns, Peter by the string quartet, the rifle shots by the kettle drum and the big drum.

Dans ce conte musical, chaque personnage est caractérisé par un motive et instrument différent: l'oiseau - flûte, la cane - hautbois, le chat - clarinette, le grand-père - basson, le loup - trois cors, Petit-Pierre - quatuor à cordes, fusils à balles - timbales et grosse caisse.

Cada una de las personas esta representada por un instrumento distinto en la orquesta: el pájaro por la flauta, el pato por el oboe, el gato por el clarinete, el abuelito por el fagote, el lobo por las tres trompas, Pedro por el cuarteto de cuerda, los tiros de los cazadores por los timbales y el bombo.

The bird
L'oiseau
El pajaro

The duck
La cane
El pato

The cat
Le chat
El gato

Grandfather
Grand-père
El abuelito

The wolf
Le loup
El lobo

Peter
Pierre
Pedro

Peter and the Wolf

Pedro y el Lobo · Pierre et le Loup

Serge Prokofieff, op. 67
Arranged for piano solo by
Thomas F. Dunhill

Early one morning Peter opened the gate and went out into the big green meadow.
Un beau matin, Pierre ouvrit la barrière et sortit dans la grande prairie verte.
Tempranito por la mañana Pedro abrió la puerta y salió al vasto y verde prado.

On the branch of a big tree sat a little bird, Peter's friend. "All is quiet," chirped the bird gaily.

Sur une des branches d'un grand arbre était assis un petit oiseau, l'ami de Pierre. Le petit oiseau pépia gaîment: "Tout est tranquille. Rien à signaler"

En la rama de un grande arbol estaba sentado un pajarito, amigo de Pedro. "Todo quieto" iba piando alegremente.

Soon a duck came waddling around. She was glad that Peter had not closed the gate, and decided to take a nice swim in the deep pond in the meadow.

A ce moment précis, un canard arriva, le nez au vent. Il était fort heureux que Pierre n'ait pas fermé la barrière, et décida de s'offrir un délicieux bain dans la mare de la prairie.

Luego salió el pato. Qué suerte que Pedro hubiera dejado abierta la puerta, pensó; y decidió darse una zambullida en la balsa del prado.

Seeing the duck, the little bird flew down upon the grass, settled next to her and shrugged his shoulders.

Apercevant le canard, le petit oiseau vola vers le gazon, se posa près de la mare et haussa frénétiquement les épaules.

Al ver el pato, el pajarito de un vuelo vino a posarse junto a él en la hierba, encongiéndose de hombros:

"What kind of bird are you, if you can't fly?" said he. To this the duck replied, "What kind of bird are you if you can't swim?" and dived . . .

"Quel drôle d'oiseau es-tu, toi qui ne sais pas voler?", dit-il. A quoi le canard répondit: "Quel drôle d'oiseau es-tu, toi qui ne sais pas nager?" et il plongea . . .

"Que clase de pájaro eres, que no sabes volar?" preguntóle. Replicó el pato: "Qué clase de pájaro eres, que no sabes nadar?"

into the pond.
dans la mare.
y zambullióse.

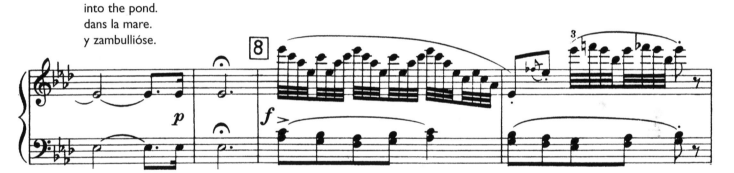

They argued and argued, the duck swimming in the pond, the little bird hopping along the shore.
Et ils discutèrent et discutèrent à l'infini, le canard plongeant dans la mare et le petit oiseau sautillant le long du bord.
Asi iban discutiendo, el pato nadando en la balsa y el pajarito saltando por los bordes.

9 Più mosso

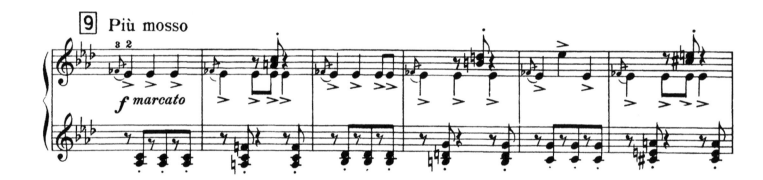

10

Suddenly something caught Peter's attention:
Tout à coup, quelque chose attira l'attention de Pierre:
De pronto, algo llamó la atención a Pedro:

He noticed a cat crawling through the grass.
C'était le chat, rampant dans les herbes du pré.
Había visto un gato arrastrándose por entre las hierbas.

11 Moderato (♩ = 104)

p

con elegansa

The cat thought: "The bird is busy arguing. I'll just grab him."

Le chat pensait: "Voilà un oiseau bien occupé à discuter. Je m'en vais l'attraper."
Pensó el gato: "El pajarito está distraido discutiendo. A ver si lo cazo."

Stealthily she crept towards him on her velvet paws.
Et furtivement, il se glissa vers l'oiseau, silencieux sur ses pattes de velours.
Y se le acercó hurtadilias con blandas pisadas.

12

"Look out!" shouted Peter and the bird immediately ...
"Attention!" cria Pierre, et immédiatement l'oiseau ...
"Cuidado!" gritó Pedro, y el pajarito ...

13 Allegro, ma non troppo (♩ = 152-160)

ff

p

flew up into the tree.
s'envola dans l'arbre.
se voló al árbol enseguida.

The duck quacked angrily at the cat from the middle of the pond.
Cependant que le canard cancannait furieusement dans la direction du chat … depuis le milieu de la mare …
Mientras el pato enojado graznaba contra el gato desde el centro de la balsa.

The cat crawled around the
Le chat tournait en rond autour
Arrastrándose en torno al

tree and thought, "Is it worth climbing up so high? By the time I get there the bird will have flown away."
de l'arbre et pensait: "Cela vaut-il la peine de grimper aussi haut? Le temps d'y arriver et cet oiseau volera plus loin."
árbol pensaba el gato: "Valdrá la pena de trepar tan alto? Al tiempo que yo llegue el pájaro se habrá volado."

Grandfather came out. He was angry
because Peter had gone to the
meadow. "It is a dangerous place. If a
wolf should come out of the forest,
then what would you do?"

Voici grand-père maintenant. Il est fâché
de ce que Pierre soit allé dans la prairie.
"C'est un endroit dangereux. Si un loup
sortait de la forêt, que ferais-tu?"

Salió el abuelito. Estaba enojado porqué
Pedro había salido al prado. "Es un lugar
peligroso. Si el lobo saliá del bosque,
qué iba a hacer el chico?"

15 **Poco più andante**

Peter paid no attention to his grandfather's words. Boys such as he are not afraid of wolves.

Pierre n'accorda aucune attention aux mots de son grand-père. Des garçons tels que lui ne craignent pas les loups.

Pedro no le hizo case el abuelito. Chices como él no le tienen miedo al lobo.

But grandfather took Peter by the hand, led him home and locked the gate.

Mais grand-père prit Pierre par la main, le conduisit à la maison et claqua la porte.

Pedro el abuelito le cogió de, la mano y se lo llevó a casa cerrando la puerta tras sí.

18 Andante

No sooner had Peter gone, than a big grey wolf came out of the forest.

A peine Pierre était-il parti qu'un énorme loup gris sortit de la forêt.

Apenas se había marchado Pedro cuando un enorme lobo gris salió del bosque.

19 Andante molto (♩ = 66)

In a twinkling the cat climbed up the tree.

En un clin d'œil, le chat grimpa dans l'arbre.

Al momento el gato se encaramó al árbol.

The duck quacked and in her excitement jumped out of the pond.

Tout cancannant, et dans une folle excitation, le canard, d'un bond, sortit de la mare.

El pato graznaba, y de puro azarado se salió de la balsa.

21 Allegro (♩ = 160)

f marcato

But no matter how hard . . .
Mais, hélas, pauvre canard . . .
Por más que procuraba . . .

p subito

the duck tried to run, she couldn't escape the wolf . . .
il avait beau courir . . .
correr el pobre pato, no podía escapar al lobo . . .

He was getting nearer . . .
Il ne pouvait échapper . . .
Ya casi le iba a alcanzar . . .

22

. . . nearer . . .
. . . au loup . . .
. . . acercándose . . .

. . . catching up with her . . .
. . . il approchait . . .
. . . más y más y más . . .

. . . attrapé . . .

cresc.

ff

and then he got her, and with one gulp swallowed her.

et tout rond d'une goulée avalé.

ya lo tiene asido y de un solo bocado lo engullió.

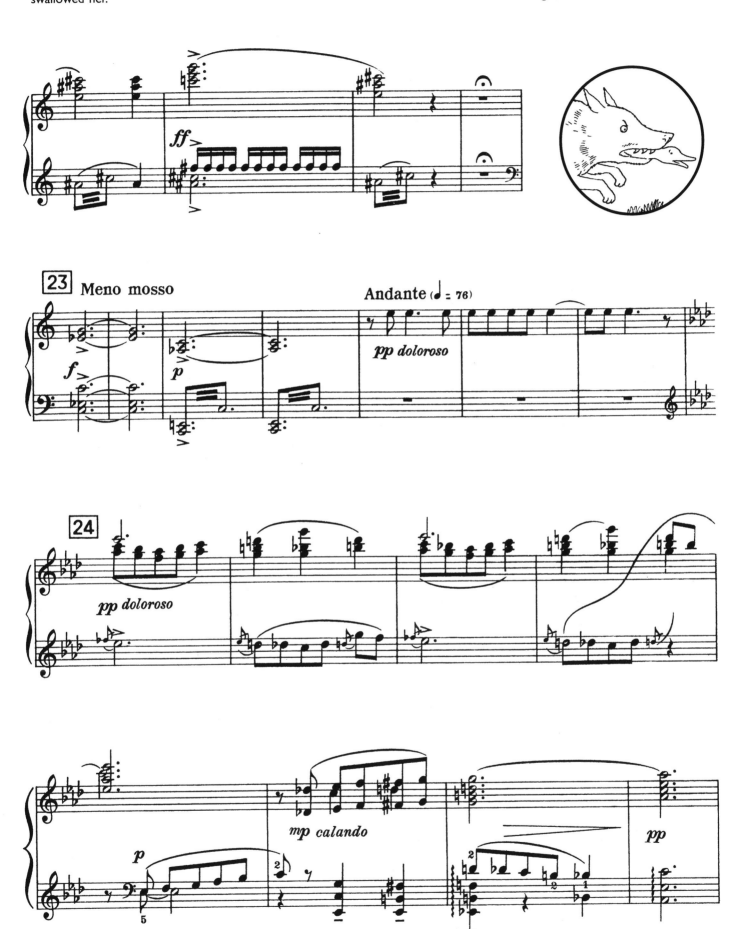

20

And now, this is how things stood: the cat was sitting on one branch . . .

Maintenant, voici la situation: le chat était assis sur une branche . . .

Y así estaban las cosas entonces: el gato sentado en una rama . . .

the bird on another . . .
l'oiseau sur une autre . . .
el pajarito en otra . . .

not too close to the cat . . .
pas trop près du chat . . .
no demasiado cerca del gato . . .

and the wolf walked round and round the tree looking at them with greedy eyes.

et le loup tournait en rond autour de l'arbre, jetant sur eux des yeux abominables.

y el lobo paseándose en derredor y lanzándoles voraces miradas.

In the meantime Peter, without the slightest fear, stood behind the closed gate watching all that was going on.

Pendant ce temps, Pierre, sans la moindre frayeur, se tenait derrière la barrière fermée, suivant les événements.

Mientras tanto Pedro, sin asomo de miedo, estaba detrás de la valla atento a cuánto iba sucediendo.

22

He ran home, took a strong rope and climbed up the high stone wall. One of the branches of the tree,
Il courut à la maison, en revint avec une forte corde et se hissa sur le haut mur de pierres. Une des branches de l'arbre
Entró corriendo en casa, tomó una solida cuerda y subióse encima de la muralla de piedra. Una de la ramas del árbol

around which the wolf was walking, stretched out over the wall.
autour duquel tournait le loup, dépassait le mur.
que el lobo iba rondando se extendía por encima de la muralla.

Grabbing hold of the branch
Attrapant la branche
Agarrándose a la rama

Peter lightly climbed over on to the tree. Pierre grimpa dans l'arbre. Pedro se encaramó con presteza el árbol.

Meno mosso

Peter said to the bird: "Fly down and circle around the wolf's head, only take care that he doesn't catch you."

Et Pierre dit à l'oiseau: "Pique, tournique, vole en rond autour de la tête du loup. Prend garde cependant qu'il ne t'attrape."

Pedro le dijo al pajarito: "Baja y vete revoloteando en torno la cabeza del lobo, pero ten cuidado que no te pille."

Vivo (♩ = 152)

The bird almost touched the wolf's head with his wings, while the wolf snapped angrily at him from this side and that.

L'oiseau en arrivait presque à toucher de ses ailes la tête du loup, cependant que le loup happait rageusement de côté et d'autre.

El pajarito casi tobaca la cabeza del lobo con sus alas mientras la bestia furiosa iba pegando dentelladas para ver si lo podía atrapar.

31 Andante molto (♩ = 66)

marcatissimo

How the bird did worry the wolf! How he wanted to catch him! But the bird was cleverer, and the wolf simply couldn't do anything about it.

Combien l'oiseau tarabustait le loup! Et combien le loup aurait voulu s'en saisir! Mais l'oiseau était le plus malin, et le loup, simplement, ne pouvait rien y faire.

Cómo le fastidiaba el pajarito! Cuánto le hubiese gustado atraparlo! Pero el pájaro era más listo y el lobo no tenía más remedio que fastidiarse.

Meanwhile Peter made a lasso and, carefully letting it down,

Pendant ce temps-là, Pierre avait fait un lasso, et, prudemment, il le laissa descendre,

Mientras tanto Pedro preparó una lazo con la cuerda y bajándolo con cuidado,

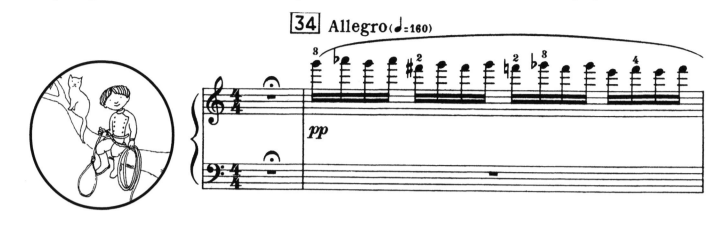

caught the wolf by the tail and pulled with all his might.

attrapa le loup par le queue, et tira de toutes ses forces.

logró pasarlo por la cola del lobo y empezó a tirar hacia sí con toda su fuerza.

Feeling himself caught, the wolf began
to jump wildly, trying to get loose.

Se sentant pris, le loup se mit à sauter
sauvagement pour se dégager.

Al sentirse preso el lobo empezó a saltar
desesperadamente para ver si se desasía.

Moderato (meno mosso)

But Peter tied the other end of the rope to the tree,
Mais Pierre avait noué à l'arbre l'autre extrémité de la corde,
Pero Pedro ató el otro cabo de la cuerda en el árbol,

36

and the wolf's jumping only made the rope round his tail tighter.
et les sauts du loup ne faisaient que resserrer le noeud qui lui prenait la queue.
y cuanto más saltaba el lobo más le apretaba la cuerda en la cola.

Just then ...
C'est alors ...
Cabalmente ...

the hunters came out of the woods
que les chasseurs sortirent du bois
los cazadoes salían del bosque

38 Allegro moderato (♩ = 116)

following the wolf's trail and shooting as they went.
suivant les traces du loup, et tirant force coups de feu en marchant.
siguiendo las huellas del lobo y disparando de vez en cuando.

But Peter, sitting in the tree, said: "Don't shoot! Birdie and I have already caught the wolf. Now help us take him to the zoo."

Mais Pierre, assis dans l'arbre, leur cria: "Ne tirez pas! Petit oiseau et moi, nous avons pris le loup. Aidez-moi, maintenant, à le transporter au jardin zoologique."

Pero Pedro encaramado en el árbol gritóles "No tiren más! Pajarito y yo hemos apresado ya el lobo. Ahora nos puenden ayudar a llevarlo al zoológico."

41 Andante ($\boldsymbol{\mathstrut}$ = 63)

And there . . .
Et maintenant . . .
Y entonces . . .

imagine the triumphant procession:
imaginez la procession triomphale:
figúrénse el cortejo triunfal:

ben ritmato
p

Peter at the head,
Pierre en tête,
Pedro a la cabeza,

44

pp

energico, ben tenuto
mf

f

f

after him the hunters leading the wolf
à sa suite, les chasseurs portant le loup
detrás de él los cazadores llevando al lobo

47 Poco più mosso (Allegro moderato) (♩ = 116)
con brio

And winding up the procession came grandfather and the cat. Grandfather tossed his head discontentedly: "Well," he said, "and if Peter hadn't caught the wolf, what then?"

Et, fermant le cortège, grand-père et le chat. Grand-père dodelinait la tête sans arrêt: "Bien, bien ... mais si Pierre n'avait pas pris le loup, que serait-il arrivé?"

Y cerrando el cortejo, el abuelito y el gato. El abuelito iba meneando la cabeza sin cesar, diciendo: "Bueno, pero si Pedro no logra entrampar al lobo, qué sucedía?"

48 Sostenuto (♩ = 100)

con eleganza

49 **L'istesso tempo**

Above them flew Birdie chirping merrily:
"My, what fine ones we are, Peter and I.
Look what we have caught!"

Au-dessus d'eux le petit oiseau volait en
pépiant plein de joie: "Seigneur! quels types
courageux nous sommes, Pierre et moi.
Voyez donc quel gibier nous avons pris!"

Por encima de ellos iba revoloteando el
pajarito, piando alegremente: "Lo
valientes que somos Pedro y yo. Ved lo
que hemos cazado!"

51 **Poco più mosso** (♩ = 112)

And if one would listen carefully, one could hear the duck quacking in the wolf's belly, because the wolf, in his hurry, had swallowed her alive.

Et si quelqu'un écoute de toutes ses oreilles, il pourra entendre le canard cancannant à l'intérieur du loup, car le loup, dans sa précipitation, avait avalé le canard vivant.

Y si uno escuchaba muy atentamente podía oir el pato graznando en la panza del lobo, pués con las prisas se lo había tragado vivo.

Printed by Halstan:
Halstan UK, 2-10 Plantation Road, Amersham, Bucks, HP6 6HJ. United Kingdom
Halstan DE, Weißliliengasse 4, 55116 Mainz. Germany